MORE THAN MONEY: THE U.S. ARMY'S FUTURE IN EUROPE

Dramatic change is sweeping through the world. The end of the war in Iraq, view of an end of American involvement in Afghanistan, regime changes in the Arab world, and financial distress around the globe have combined to force adjustments to the United States' international footprint and future defense strategies. Seizing on these and other situations, opponents to America's presence in Europe have called for a complete removal of American ground troops and a reexamination of the U.S. approach to military commitments to European partners in the European Union and the North Atlantic Treaty Organization.

As history has illustrated, American presence in Europe, or lack thereof, has played a significant role in the security situation on the European continent for nearly 100 years. Adjustments to that presence are natural and obligatory of a nation confronting an altered global security environment and looking to improve its fiscal outlook. Complete removal of American ground troops from Europe is a mistake, however. It would greatly reduce the effectiveness of America's military and the defense capabilities of U.S. partners, and most importantly, it would indicate a dramatic step back from American leadership in the world.

In January 2012, President Barack Obama and Secretary of Defense Leon Panetta, unveiled a new defense strategy to meet fiscal constraints and maintain American partnerships, alliances, and forward presence in the world. Recognizing a need to adjust emphasis to the Pacific, the strategy reprioritized

American military presence from other, less volatile regions, such as Europe and Latin America, to the Pacific.[1] This shift is appropriate based on current international conditions, while signifying a continued commitment to European partners.

This paper will analyze in detail the costs and benefits of American ground troop presence on the European continent. It concludes that the plan put forward by the President and Secretary of Defense for the future disposition of U.S. Army personnel in Europe is both sensible and cost-effective. It will begin by examining the history of American presence in Europe and the primary threats that drove such presence. Next, the paper will outline the main arguments that critics have offered against sustaining a military presence in Europe. Through an examination of the current world situation and the roles that American forces in Europe play today, it will then identify important weaknesses in each of those arguments—weaknesses that lead one to conclude that retaining a significant force in Europe will be crucial to security in Europe and the Middle East as well as to the US position in world affairs. That does not mean that the United States and its European partners cannot do better, however; the paper ends with recommendations for increased American-European military interoperability that could further enhance operational readiness and international security.

It is important to note that decisions on continued American presence in Europe were announced in early 2012. Specifically, United States Army Europe (USAREUR) will reduce the current brigade combat team totals from four to two between 2012 and 2014.[2] The paper finds that these decisions are significant and appropriate.

Good Intentions, Failed Presence: Between the World Wars

President Woodrow Wilson was the first U.S. president to truly seek a larger role for the United States in Europe. Understanding economic and diplomatic relationships with Europe had been in existence since the creation of the country 125 years earlier, Wilson recognized the importance of American interests outside the borders of the U.S., specifically related to interactions with the European continent. His immediate concerns were relative to an expanding Germany and were in line with those of earlier statesmen, Theodore Roosevelt among them, who believed increased German power would pose a direct threat to American interests in the Western Hemisphere.[3]

Fighting off the echoed warnings of George Washington to avoid entanglements in Europe, Wilson urged Congress and the country to increase its role in the international security situation developing across the Atlantic. Even before American involvement in World War I Wilson commented, "No covenant of cooperative peace that does not include the peoples of the New World can suffice to keep the future safe against war."[4] Following the war his efforts to connect the United States and Europe foresaw an understanding that American involvement was crucial to maintaining the peace.

American participation in World War I was the first military venture onto the European continent and Wilson and others saw American involvement in Europe as vital to continued peace and security on the continent. The proposed establishment of the League of Nations and the Versailles Treaty were both seen by Wilson as critical to not only future American security, but security around the globe. Ultimately, however, the U.S. Congressional rejection of the League and the treaty would continue the pre-war status quo. Rather than see the imperative of American involvement in the affairs of Europe, the United States reverted behind the barrier provided by the Atlantic Ocean and returned to watching European affairs from a distance.

The rise of Hitler's Germany, continued diminishment of power in Britain and France, and the repression of the Soviet Union failed to rouse U.S. interests in engaging more closely with Europe. Although simple participation in the League of Nations is no guarantee war would have been avoided in 1939, a failure to participate by the United States eliminated any real ability to influence the direction European powers were heading. The ultimate conflict that engulfed the world for a second time was something for which the U.S. simply had little voice to prevent.

The Cold War and a Change in American Stature

Cessation of hostilities between the Axis and Allied Powers in Europe in May 1945 and Japan three months later changed the stature of America forever. Once able to manage affairs within its own borders, the United States was now a global leader and was looked to by all others as one of the two great powers of the world.

With its partners in Europe, the United States provided the counterbalance to the Soviet Union's expansion throughout eastern Europe and immediately became the key to preventing further Soviet influence in the western European countries. Even as Britain and France occupied pieces of Germany, however, it was well understood that the true hegemonic power in Europe was the United States.[5]

U.S. economic might shouldered the substantial burdens of resourcing the war, though the populations of Europe suffered a great deal more than the American people. In the end, it was the factories of America that turned the tide in the war. It was appropriate then that the Marshall Plan and subsequent appropriations of more than $13 billion would stimulate the economic recovery of the European continent and foster continued European integration and U.S. involvement in the affairs of Europe. Indeed, having invested in the financial recovery of the continent, the U.S. sought a continually evolving European integration that could both counter Soviet influence and a lessen requirements for direct U.S. involvement.[6]

A lack of U.S. involvement was not something hoped for by the western European powers. Ultimately only America's participation and leadership in forming the North Atlantic Treaty Organization (NATO) would be the impetus for continued strengthening of European integration.

The creation of NATO would do what many Europeans hoped for: keep America in Europe and help to foster continued security on the European Continent. In fact, as Lord Lionel Ismay, British general and diplomat and future Secretary General of NATO noted, the alliance was designed to "keep the Russians out, the Americans in and the Germans down."[7] Most importantly, early American commitment to NATO provided the leadership and security necessary to permit the full implementation of the Marshall Plan's infusion of financial capital and industrial capacity.

On the security front, NATO's role in Europe and counter to the Soviet Union gained strength throughout its first 40 years. Americans at home realized the importance of the alliance and saw the possibility of future conflict with the Soviet Union playing out on the fields of Europe and not the American plains. European leaders, likewise, realized the value of American soldiers on the continent, feeling that American presence signified a legitimate sharing of the burdens associated with what often seemed like certain conflict.

Initial angst was raised as a result of what appeared to be Europe taking advantage of U.S. defense of the continent while raising political and economic differences with America. U.S. involvement in Vietnam, for instance, provided a galvanizing topic for Europeans. Demonstrating large opposition to American involvement in Southeast Asia, Europeans voiced their opinions while sitting beneath a shield of American protection in their homelands. Some Americans seized on European two-side arguments to call for a return of American troops or an increase in the European portion of security spending on the continent.[8]

In early 1974, President Richard Nixon highlighted the dichotomy during a discussion with American businessmen, "They (Europe) cannot have the United States participation and cooperation on the security front and then proceed to have confrontation and even hostility on the economic and political front."[9]

The demand for increased burden-sharing by America's European partners continued well into the 1980s. These arguments were often used by American politicians to call for a return of American troops to the continental United States.[10]

Recognizing the validity of these discussions, American politicians over time worked continually to increase European integration. Believing further integration of Europe would lead to increased economic capacity and defense abilities, U.S. politicians sought to placate concerns at home while working to strengthen Europe's evolving economic and political institutions.

Throughout these times of discussion, argument, and desire for equal burden-sharing, there remained a constant hegemonic balance, however. As a result of the Soviet Union's continued military building and presence in eastern Europe, the calls for the return of American troops to the United States were often moot. Changes to the bipolar state of the world engendered change to the American situation in Europe.

Europe After the Cold War

The collapse of the Soviet Union and the Warsaw Pact changed the world's perspective overnight. Where a balance of power had previously existed, the lack of possible Soviet armies attacking through Europe altered the view of American presence on the European continent. As Michael Klare noted, "the end of the Cold War swept away the likelihood of a high-intensity conflict in Europe, and with it the sole justification for maintenance of heavy, well-equipped forces."[11]

This viewpoint and America's new standing as the unipolar power in the world produced struggles to determine the future world environment. Whether termed a "New World Order" or a period of "Pax Americana," the ten years following the end of the Cold War lacked the stability afforded by the Cold War. The result was a significant number of military actions undertaken by the United States and its allies in various portions of the world. Specific to NATO and Europe was the conflict in the Balkans which ignited in 1991 and provided a challenge for U.S. and European nations which the Cold War had long prevented.

The experience of the war in the Balkans highlighted to need to redefine the American relationship to Europe and determine the applicability of future security requirements on the European continent and throughout the world. Recognizing this need, NATO worked to incorporate former members of the Soviet bloc into the alliance and, by the turn of the century, had increased membership in the alliance to include Poland, Hungary, and the Czech Republic. Nine additional members were added following the turn of the century, bringing the total NATO membership to 28.[12]

In the 20 years since the end of the Cold War, Europe and the United States have worked to improve security through continued partnerships and alliances. NATO and the European Union have each worked to foster enhanced European security while each has worked with the United States to increase economic and security aspects around the globe.

Specific to security, NATO participation in the wars in Afghanistan and

Libya has greatly increased the interoperability of U.S. and European militaries and highlighted the strength offered by continued American involvement on the European continent.

While European security seems to have improved since the fall of the Soviet Union, fears of Russian future intentions continue to concern European nations, specifically the countries of the former Warsaw Pact. The Russian attack of the Republic of Georgia in 2008, for instance, provided an example of action many eastern European nations find concerning.[13] Additionally, on-going fears of Iranian nuclear proliferation and the potential of a nuclear-Iran to launch missiles at the European continent have raised concerns for continued European security.[14]

Changes in American Ground Troop Presence Over Time

Prior to the Second World War, no American ground troops were permanently based on the European continent. That changed with the defeat of the Axis Powers and subsequent partitioning of Germany. Immediately following the cessation of the war, 1.6 million Americans were stationed in Europe, with the large majority performing duties as an occupation force in the American sector of West Germany.[15]

At the time of NATO's establishment and throughout the majority of the Cold War period, an average of 250,000 soldiers were stationed in Europe, with individual garrisons located in England, France, Germany, and Italy. As in previous years, the majority of ground troops were located in Germany. In 1961, as a response to the Berlin Wall crisis, additional ground forces were deployed to Europe, bringing the total to a high of 277,000.[16]

The largest reduction in European-stationed ground troops was following the end of the Cold War and post-Operation Desert Storm. As a result of the Soviet Union's demise and the financial necessity to reduce overall military end strength, forces in Europe were drastically reduced from 213,000 to 122,000.[17]

On September 11, 2001, when terrorists attacked the World Trade Center and Pentagon, there were approximately 62,000 American ground troops stationed in Europe, with the majority of those forces in Germany. Over the ten years that followed the 9/11 attacks, the Army's force structure in Europe, specifically Germany, evolved dramatically, as one division headquarters returned to the United States leaving four combat brigades and sustainment organizations totaling approximately 42,000 soldiers.[18]

<u>Arguments for the Removal of American Forces</u>

To be certain, calls for removal of U.S. ground forces in Europe are not a recent occurrence. Similar to the arguments used to keep Americans out of Europe following World War I, opponents of American presence on the European continent have been constant and oft apparent.

In most cases, the loudest calls for a removal of ground forces in Europe have come in two circumstances: fiscal problems at home and periods of military conflict weariness. American politicians have routinely used these two situations in combination with the knowledge there is no U.S. constituency for overseas bases to provide emphasis and gain traction in their pursuits to return American troops to the continental United States.

As noted earlier, over the past 60 years, many different political leaders have called for American retrenchment. From the initial opposition of the Marshall Plan by Senator Robert Taft in the 1940's, through Senator Mike Mansfield's calls for reductions through the Mutual Balanced Force Reduction Program (MBFR) in the early 1970's, to current calls from politicians such as Representatives Ron Paul and Barney Frank, the ability to rally Americans to support reductions and removals of troops from Europe is always one with few costs to politicians.[19] Simply put, removing forces from Europe sounds appealing to the average American who would prefer to spend money on programs within the United States as opposed to outside U.S. borders.

Adding to the political debate associated with such pronouncements are the academic discussions focusing on a number of specific reasons for retrenchment. First, and foremost, are the arguments pertaining to money and budgets. Based on the continued reductions of European financial contributions to defense spending, America is taking on more than its fair share of the security contributions. Pundits believe this money, spent on American troops stationed in Europe, could be better spent at home. Additionally, until America stops spending on security in Europe, Europeans will not increase their defense contributions.[20] As will be noted later, there is no indication that such increases in European spending will occur in the absence of American military presence.

Added to the failure of European partners to shoulder their share of the defense burden, advocates of retrenchment note the lack of a credible reason for Americans to be positioned in Europe. Following the Second World War it was the rebuilding of Europe that required significant American presence. As Europe developed, focus shifted to countering the threat of communism and the Soviet Union. After the Cold War ended, argue retrenchment proponents, threats to Europe no longer justified positioning Americans on European soil.[21]

A third line of reasoning cited by proponents of retrenchment policies is that American leadership in the world is not a requirement for European or international security. In fact, say those in favor of retrenchment, the belief that "someone has to do it" or no one will is not a reason for America to maintain its overseas burdens.[22]

Next, and in line with George Washington's advice to avoid foreign entanglements, retrenchment proponents note U.S. participation in alliances such as NATO actually makes the nation more vulnerable. The forward presence of American soldiers provides an easier target for its enemies and the requirements to assist others in alliances makes it more likely that the United States will be involved in hostilities in those regions.[23]

One final argument noted by those opposed to continued American presence in Europe, and the remainder of the world, is the argument of security through geography. This argument is one most closely aligned to former isolationist positions and claims that the vast oceans to the east and west of the U.S. provide the greatest security from a party hostile to the United States.

Those who espouse this argument note the two oceans provide not only a physical but also a mental barrier to America's enemies.[24]

In all cases, retrenchment advocates note the U.S. strength in force projection capabilities. There is simply no place in the world that American force cannot be exerted within a tolerable amount of time.[25]

Each of these arguments has strings of truth and, when used by politicians speaking to home constituencies experiencing high unemployment and general dissatisfaction with America's position in the world relative to its European partners, redeploying American troops from Europe seems like a quick way to make things better financially and with regards to security. Noting the United States could, "…save tens of billions of dollars a year by curtailing our commitment to the defense of Western Europe," Congressman Barney Frank has used these points to call for American retrenchment.[26] When viewed together, these arguments miss the mark, however.

Money: Low Costs and Significant Benefits

Arguably, America's fiscal future is calamitous, and current economic situation is the worst in decades. With a continually growing $14 trillion debt, social security, Medicare, and Medicaid costs increasing annually, and a high national unemployment rate, the federal government must seek every avenue to cut costs and raise revenues. As it applies to cost cutting, the Budget Control Act of 2011 demands cuts to U.S. defense spending of nearly $500 billion over the next ten years, relative to the plan the Department of Defense submitted to Congress in February 2011. If the law is not changed, then additional cuts

13

totaling another one-half trillion dollars over the decade will automatically take effect, beginning in January 2013.[27]

The Department of Defense has embraced the first round of budgetary reductions, but the Secretary of Defense argues that the automated cuts that would begin in January 2013 are untenable. In line with the first round of cuts put in place through the Budget Control Act, the Department of Defense adopted new strategic guidance, articulated in the budget materials delivered to Congress in February 2012. Limiting defense spending responsibly is the current priority of the Department of Defense (DoD), which is working diligently to maintain the effectiveness of the current force. As President Obama pledged in his cover letter to the guidance, "I am determined that we meet the challenges of this moment responsibly and that we emerge even stronger in a manner that preserves American global leadership, maintains our military superiority and keeps faith with our troops, military families, and veterans."[28]

Although accurate figures are debated in discussions of American presence, the U.S. Army asserts current spending in Europe is approximately $1.2 billion annually to sustain the four brigade combat teams in Germany and Italy, a combat aviation brigade, engineer, sustainment, medical service units, and associated unit headquarters.[29] The benefits of this relatively small force presence are substantial. Over the past ten years, the U.S. Army Europe (USAREUR) has averaged between 30 and 40 percent of its soldiers deployed in support of operations in Iraq or Afghanistan.[30] Simultaneous to combat deployments, USAREUR has continued the critical mission of global engagement with its partners in Europe, training and preparing our forces for combat and other operations in partnership with European countries that are NATO members and those that do not belong to the alliance. The return on these training partnerships is significant, with many of those partners providing force contributions to the International Assistance Security Forces (ISAF) mission in Afghanistan.

Specifically, between 2010 and 2011, USAREUR partnered with 28 nations, training in 11 separate countries, and conducted 21 major exercises.[31] These exercises strengthened interoperability between the various nations and forged a bond that enhanced the conduct of combat operations in Afghanistan. One such partnership was that established between the 2nd Stryker Cavalry Regiment (SCR) and the Romanian Army. During training missions in Romania in 2009, the 2 SCR initiated a relationship that continued between 2010 and 2011 in Zabul Province, Afghanistan, where both organizations served side by side for a year of combat operations. What began as simple platoon and company training operations bloomed into cooperation between brigade and battalion headquarters in a combat zone. Ultimately, the Romanian Army assumed complete responsibility for one Afghan district, as a result.[32]

Those wishing to see America's presence eliminated in Europe make little of such partnerships and troop contributions. They often argue that aside from the large national contributions from England, France, and Germany, the impact of such troop deployments is insignificant.[33] This could not be further from the truth as the total contribution of nations from Europe is near 40,000 soldiers.[34] Of that 40,000, less than half are from the United Kingdom, Germany, and France, and all of the functions are critical to continued operations in Afghanistan. As an example of the significance of the international contribution, on one small forward operating base in Uruzgan Province, the main installation security is provided by the Slovakian Army, and intelligence and police augmentees from England, France, and the Netherlands provide significant enhancements to the combined U.S. and Australian headquarters. Without such commitments, the United States would require sizable increases in force presence to accomplish the same missions.[35]

Aside from the specific troop contributions to on-going U.S. combat operations, the interoperability achieved through partner training and combat has enabled additional efficiencies for future security contingencies. Action in Libya proved the value of such connections, even if the interoperabilities were those related to the use of air power and creation of partnerships. Despite hurdles encountered during the Libyan campaign, the familiarity of nations under the NATO umbrella and the commitment formed through operations in Afghanistan and training events in Europe proved vital to the defeat of the Libyan government. [36] Tactics, techniques, and procedures, in addition to military doctrine have all increased the combat effectiveness of the partnerships and established a genuine connection between the American military and its European partners.

In addition to the partner training and combat abilities attributable to American presence in Europe, the critical transportation and medical benefits of a forward positioning have been instrumental to American power for quite some time. In the past ten years, alone, the ability to move personnel and equipment through the major hubs in Europe enroute to the combat theaters of the Middle East has been instrumental to continuous operations. Additionally, and perhaps more important, the Landstuhl Regional Medical Center's location in Germany has literally saved lives on a near daily basis. Since 2004, Landstuhl has provided treatment for more than 65,000 patients from the conflict zones of Iraq and Afghanistan, including patients from 45 nations. Specific to combat casualties, the medical center has treated well over 12,000 patients with a survival rate in excess of 99 percent.[37] In the case of both power projection and medical care, it is physically possible to transport people and casualties around the world without landing. With American refueling assets it is unnecessary to stop to or from the United States. The long-term requirements for such travel are substantial, however. Medical procedures requiring immediate attention are possible only because Landstuhl is within hours of current and potential combat zones in the Middle East. Obtaining landing rights in or air access through countries not in favor of U.S. policies would also add to the difficulties associated with travel of extensive distances. These concerns are all dramatically mitigated through U.S. continued presence in Europe.

Finally, opponents of American presence on the European continent are quick to point to Europe's comparably paltry financial contribution to defense. Pointing to NATO's, "Prague Capabilities Commitment," agreed to in 2002 and requiring each nation to spend 2% of its GDP on defense, those wishing to see

U.S. military forces return from Europe note Europeans will not increase their contributions as long as American forces are present to defend Europe.[38]

While it is true that fewer than 5 of the 28 NATO countries contribute 2% or greater of their GDP, this requirement is misleading.[39] Retrenchment proponents note the United States spends nearly 5% of its GDP on defense and compare that contribution to European spending. The comparisons fail to recognize the scope of American interests in comparison to that of the European powers, however. For example, there is little reason to expect a country such as Latvia to have the same defense inclinations as the United States. Aside from specific European concerns, Latvia has no compelling reason to spend on a comparable rate with the United States, which is concerned with security in all corners of the globe.

Additionally, there is no guarantee countries would increase their defense commitments should American presence be eliminated. In fact, as U.S. ground troops in Europe have declined over the past 20 years, there has been no corresponding increase in European defense spending. Rather, the opposite has been true. If this were to remain the case, the elimination of American troops in Europe would only reduce the total emphasis of defense forces on the continent.[40]

A World Without Leadership

In 2007, then-presidential candidate Barack Obama stated America, "...can neither retreat from the world nor bully it into submission. We must lead the world, by deed and example."[41] With this in mind, American leadership is one of the most vital aspects of maintaining ground troops in Europe.

As noted earlier, America's lack of European presence between the two world wars muted any voice the U.S. may have wanted to prevent war in Europe in the 1940's. Conversely, following World War II, America's voice was resounding and allowed it to provide direction related to international security.

Over the 40 years that followed the Second World War, America's example provided hope to portions of the world living under oppressive regimes. Perhaps America's greatest power is the ability to influence through the examples of tolerance, representative democracy, and liberty. In a unipolar or multipolar world, it is imperative that such examples continue.

Retrenchment from Europe would eliminate the feeling that America was a true part of the security discussion. European partners, though still aware of American power, would be less likely to heed the leadership attempts of the United States. In the present situation, it is possible for Americans to claim a shared burden with regards to troops on the ground in Europe. This common experience gives the United States more than a simple vote when it comes to discussions with Europe. America can wield influence from its position of military presence.

The situation with Iran provides an excellent case in point. With regards to influencing European attitudes towards Iran, the United States can look to its sharing of risk. That is, the presence of American soldiers in a location that could be under the threat of a nuclear Iran gives America the ability to influence

European reaction with shared concerns. Without Americans in a position of risk, the United States approach to European pressures is reduced to asking Europeans for a favor.

Maintaining a legitimate voice with European nations through continued presence and shared hardship, the United States is more able to provide leadership that enables the achievement of national interests. Incorporating a transformational leadership style, America can provide a vision that is in the best interests of both international security and the future of the United States. As noted by Dr. Michael Parent and Dr. R. Brent Gallupe in their study of leadership on group support systems, "Transformational leaders…motivate followers to do more than they originally expected by raising levels of consciousness, getting followers to transcend self-interests for the sake of the group or organization, and by raising need levels by adding the need for self-actualization to the need for recognition."[42] This is precisely what is possible through continued American presence and participation in Europe.

In Samuel Huntington's major work, *The Clash of Civilizations and the Remaking of World Order*, he notes the criticality of such leadership, specifically with our European partners:

> "In the aftermath of the Cold War the United States became consumed with massive debates over the proper course of American foreign policy. In this era, however, the United States can neither dominate nor escape the world. Neither internationalism nor isolationism, neither multilateralism nor unilateralism, will best serve its interests. Those will best be advanced by eschewing these opposing extremes and instead adopting an Atlanticist policy of closer cooperation with its European partners to protect and advance the interest and value of the unique civilization they share."[43]

Return of American troops from Europe eliminates this "Atlanticist" bond. Although the United States retains a connection with Europeans, it returns to the type of relationship that preceded the Second World War. In areas America wishes to exert influence on Europe it will have to hope the Europeans feel inclined to agree. There is no shared risk, such as that provided by a nuclear Iran, that enables America to provide additional influence or pressure.

<u>Vulnerability Versus Capability</u>

In his Farewell Address in 1796, President George Washington noted,

> "Europe has a set of primary interests which to us have none; or a very remote relation. Hence she must be engaged in frequent controversies, the causes of which are essentially foreign to our concerns. Hence, therefore, it must be unwise in us to implicate ourselves by artificial ties in the ordinary vicissitudes of her politics, or the ordinary combinations and collisions of her friendships or enmities."[44]

Washington's comments have often been referenced with a forewarning of attachment to Europe and foreign alliances, in general. Comparisons of today with the world situation in 1796 are far from valid, however. The interconnected world of the present makes Washington's comments out of date and context. Our reliance on various organizations around the world fosters increased influence and enhances American interests.

Specific to the NATO alliance, our contributions to the group have been paid back handsomely in the past ten years. Article V of the North Atlantic Treaty calls on each of the member nations to come to the aid of any that are attacked.[45] In the 60 years since its signing, Article V has only been implemented one time: on 9/11. A treaty written primarily to stave off a seemingly imminent Soviet invasion of Europe was employed instead to offer support to the greatest military power of the alliance. Retrenchment proponents claim U.S. connections to such alliances will result in our requirement to come to the aid of others, yet the opposite has been the case.

Since the end of the Second World War, only U.S. action in Korea based on support of South Korea and the United Nations and operations in the Balkans are truly the result of military commitments to an external nation or alliance. The remainder of the multitude of military operations executed since 1945 have been the result of American concerns with national interests.[46]

The presence of American ground troops in Europe does not increase chances for military action. In fact, the forward presence of those troops serves as a deterrent to possible aggression in not only Europe but the areas within the influence of those soldiers, notably Africa and the Middle East.[47]

Isolating or Insulating

Since the beginning of U.S. history, geography has certainly been an ally of the nation. The separation from European and Pacific powers over the past 200 years provided greater defenses than large defending armies. The depth provided by the Atlantic and Pacific Oceans has long since been bridged by the rocket engine and the disguised terrorist.

Retrenchment arguments for the return of troops to the continental United States cite the use of our natural geography as the main defense from foreign

22

incursions. Further, they argue American troops positioned in Europe provide an easy target for terrorists and others wishing to strike Americans.[48] Both these points of view are incorrect and fail to understand the global reach of America's adversaries, both national and transnational threats.

9/11 provides proof of America's new vulnerability. The greatest terrorist attack against Americans was in the continental United States, not against an American entity overseas. Although these are the most visible and successful terrorist attacks, there have been others and multiple attempts since the end of the Cold War.[49]

Additionally, the threat to the United States is not limited to terrorist organizations. Missile advancements in North Korea have enabled a breach of the Pacific Ocean's protections. Additionally, evidence of Iranian efforts to conduct attacks on U.S. soil are many and growing everyday.[50]

The Way Ahead: Recommendations for Greater Efficiencies

With decisions already made concerning America's future footprint in Europe, the real questions concern how the United States maintains the current levels of interoperability with the international military community and how America continues to show its commitment to international and European security. Answers to these questions are available in the future footprint of U.S. forces in Europe and the way interactions, training and otherwise, occur with U.S. and European militaries.

Multinational Brigades and basing in Europe and the United States

Operations in Afghanistan over the past ten years have proven the effectiveness of fighting alongside international allies. That said, the ability to attain particular levels of interoperability have come through experience rather than prior training. Such interoperability has been attained through combined exercises at the Joint Maneuver Training Center at Grafenwoehr, Germany, and partner exercises throughout Europe.[51]

Combined exercises and operations have significantly increased interoperability in Afghanistan, in particular, and provided for strong relationships between numerous militaries throughout the European continent. Training events in Romania, Bulgaria, the Republic of Georgia, and other nations have provided for enhanced relationships and strengthened bonds both in and out of Afghanistan.[52]

The creation of multiple multinational brigades will further increase such interaction and maintain interoperability and functioning relationships after US and allied combat troops leave Afghanistan. The locations of these brigades could do even more to foster such continued connections.

Much has been written in the past about multinational military organizations, and the current EuroCorps, NATO Response Force, and EU Rapid Reaction Force provide examples of current thoughts or practices. In nearly all cases, the units themselves have been either paper armies, used to supply personnel to headquarters organizations, or employed in non-hostile environments. The EuroCorps, for instance, though consisting of dedicated military units from France and Germany, has failed to deploy to any type of contingency or combat operation. In effect, the EuroCorps has been symbolic in nature.[53]

Similarly, the NATO Response Force and EU Rapid Reaction Force consist of forces that are "dedicated" to the designated force but do not live and train together on a standard basis. Rather, in the event of a crisis situation, the units dedicated to the organization are to be mobilized for action under the respective force.[54]

To overcome these inadequacies, two multinational brigades should be formed with dedicated forces from each of the European nations and the United States. The size of the contribution to the brigade is less concerning than the requirement that each nation participate. In addition, there should be no national caveats that prevent the deployment of forces or limit the use of any nation's military contribution to the brigades.

Command of the brigades should rotate between nations with a requirement from all nations' forces to take orders from the commander without debate. Concerns about national preferences can be mitigated by the provision of a deputy brigade commander from a different nation and creation of fully multinational staffs.

Organization of the brigade should be in line with the American Brigade Combat Team table of organization and equipment as it relates to numbers and types of units, with three infantry battalions, one reconnaissance squadron, a field artillery battalion, and a support battalion. Each of the battalions should be one nationality to enable the parent nation to outfit the organization based on its type (e.g., infantry or support). Specialty organizations such as the military intelligence company, signal company, engineer company, anti-tank company, military police platoon and unmanned aerial vehicle platoon would also be provided by separate nations, enabling even the smallest militaries in Europe to provide forces. Where specialty positions may be necessary, such as intelligence or communications specialists, specific augmentees could be appointed. Such alignment of the multinational brigades adheres to the spirit within the Smart Defense concept and allows the United States to "pool, share, and specialize capabilities as needed to meet 21st century challenges."[55]

Billeting of the units provides an opportunity to increase burden sharing and enable additional American participation in Europe with reduced costs. This is accomplished by housing one of the brigades at the Grafenwoehr Military Community, in Germany, and one brigade at Fort Bragg, North Carolina. In each case, training areas abound to enable excellent training opportunities and billeting space is enabled through U.S. Army reductions. Both locations also provide exceptional access to transportation hubs, specifically rail and air.[56]

The basing of a multinational brigade in the United States is perhaps the greatest commitment to European partners and indicates an emphasis on the part of the U.S. to continue enhancing relationships and military interoperability. Understanding the details of such a relationship are many and national negotiations critical to creation of such organizations, sufficient energy should be invested to create such units. The benefits of these connections are enormous in comparison with the costs related to time and money.

Of course, creation of the brigades is a waste of effort and finances should they remain unemployed. As a result, each brigade should assume a rotational readiness to allow one to deploy while the other trains and refits. Furthermore, the brigades should be employed at the first opportunity to strengthen the capability and increase both the unit's confidence and the international understanding of their importance.

Exercise Rotations and Technological Exploitation

The U.S. Department of Defense has indicated an emphasis on increased American participation in exercises on the European continent.[57] This rotational model permits units not normally associated with European armies to interact and train with possible future allies. Such rotational training events will assist in maintaining the interoperability gained through combat action over the past ten years and provide a continued example of American commitment to European and international security.

These exercises, which engender visions of the former REFORGER exercises of the Cold War, should work to leverage available technologies to increase participation while reducing costs.[58] Use of the Live, Virtual, and Constructive model provide opportunities to use actual soldiers and organizations and virtually link staffs and leadership organizations to simultaneous operations.[59] Such abilities are already in use in the United States Army and have provided significant training benefits at reduced financial costs.

By implementing such a strategy and a rotational mindset, the impacts on the environment, fiscal policy, and public opinion can be minimized while attaining significant increases in international training levels.

Conclusion

American presence on the European continent has provided for 60 years of relative peace. In addition, it has enhanced American foreign policy in Europe and throughout the world, while providing the United States with a forward location critical to military operations in remote corners of the globe.

Acknowledging reductions to that footprint are fiscally responsible and possible based on the European security situation, maintaining American ground troops in Europe provides the United States with a continued voice in European politics, maintains critical military interoperability between the American and European militaries, and indicates a continued commitment by the United States to provide global leadership for the future.

Endnotes

[1] Department of Defense, "Sustaining U.S. Global Leadership: Priorities for 21st Century Defense," (January 2012): 1-8.

[2] Jennifer Svan and John VanDiver, "Panetta: 2 Army Combat Brigades Will Leave Europe," *Stars and Stripes* (January 13, 2012).

[3] Michael Lind, *The American Way of Strategy*, (New York: Oxford University Press, 2006): 114.

[4] Woodrow Wilson, "Remarks to Congress," January 1917, http://www.firstworldwar.com/source/peacewithoutvictory.htm (accessed January 24, 2012).

[5] Lind, *The American Way of Strategy*, 115.

[6] George C. Marshall, "Remarks at Harvard", June 5, 1947, http://www.usaid.gov/multimedia/video/marshall/marshallspeech.html

[7] Geir Lunestad, *'Empire' by Integration*, (New York: Oxford University Press, 1998): 167.

[8] Lawrence S. Kaplan, *NATO Divided, NATO United: The Evolution of an Alliance*, (Westport, CT: Praeger Publishers, 2004): 50-51.

[9] Lundestad, *'Empire' by Integration*, 102.

[10] Flora Lewis, "European Defense Dilemma," *New York Times, April 5, 2005*, pp. A.23-A.23. http://search.proquest.com/docview/425782394?accountid=4444 (accessed March 9, 2012); Richard Halloran, "Pentagon report says allies fail to bear share of military burden," *New York Times* (August 2, 1982), pp. A.4-A.4. Retrieved from http://search.proquest.com/docview/424413194?accountid=4444 (accessed March 9, 2012); Kaplan, NATO Divided, NATO United, 62-63; Time, "The Nation: The Pros and Cons of NATO Troop WIthdrawl," May 24, 1971, http://www.time.com/time/printout/0,8816, 905070,00.html (accessed September 27, 2011).

[11] Michael T. Klare, "U.S. Military Policy in the Post-Cold War Era," *The Socialist Register, 1992*, http://socialistregister.com/index.php/srv/article/view/5611 (accessed February 3, 2012).

[12] North Atlantic Treat Organization, "Member States," http://www.nato.int/cps/en/natolive/topics_52044.htm (accessed February 10, 2012).

[13] Tymoshenko, Yulia. (2007). Containing Russia. *Foreign Affairs, 86*(3), 69-69.

[14] Reuters.com, "Israel: Iran Will Have U.S.-Range Missile in 2-3 Years," http://www.reuters.com/assets/print?aid=USTRE81L1B420120222 (accessed February 23, 2012).

[15] Earl F. Ziemke, *The U.S. Army in the Occupation of Germany: 1944-1946*, (Washington, DC: U.S. Army Center of Military History, 1990): 320.

[16] U.S. Army Europe Web Site, "History," http://www.eur.army.mil/organization/history.htm (accessed January 25, 2012).

[17] U.S. Army Europe Web Site, "History," http://www.eur.army.mil/organization/history.htm (accessed January 25, 2012).

[18] Department of Defense Website, "Military Personnel Statistics," http://siadapp.dmdc.osd.mil/personnel/MILITARY/miltop.htm (accessed January 25, 2012); These figures consist of American ground troops on the European continent, with the large majority being U.S. Army personnel. The troops were stationed throughout the continent with the primacy being in Germany and Italy. The numbers include all personnel who were assigned to Europe at the end of the fiscal year (September 30).

[19] Time, "The Nation: The Pros and Cons of NATO Troop WIthdrawl," May 24, 1971, http://www.time.com/time/printout/0,8816, 905070,00.html (accessed September 27, 2011).

Tomas Valesek, "Defence Spending: A Race to the Bottom," August 24, 2011, http://www.publicserviceeurope.com/article/764/defence-spending-a-race-to-the-bottom (accessed March 9, 2012).

[20] Mike Coffman, "How to Cut the Defense Budget," Denver Post, September 04, 2011, http://www.denverpost.com/opinion/ci_18808717 (accessed October 14, 2011).

[21] Paul K. MacDonald and Joseph M. Parent, "The Wisdom of Retrenchment," Foreign Affairs 90, no. 6 (November 2011): 1-6 http://vnweb.hwwilsonweb.com/ezproxy.usawcpubs.org/hww/results/results_single_ftPES.jhtml (accessed December 14, 2011).

[22] Benjamin H. Friedman, Eugene Gholz, Daryl G. Press, and Harvey M. Sapolsky, "Restraining Order For Strategic Modesty," World Affairs, Fall 2009, pp 84-94.

[23] Ibid, 84-94.

[24] Ibid, 84-94; John J. Mearsheimer, *The Tragedy of Great Power Politics* (New York: Norton), 2001: 44.

[25] Ibid, 84-94.

[26] Barney Frank, "How to Save the Global Economy: Cut Defense Spending," Foreign Policy, Jan/Feb 2012, http://www.foreignpolicy.com/articles/2012/01/03/4_cut_defense_spending (accessed March 9, 2012).

[27] Congressional Budget Office web site, "Discretionary Spending Under the Budget Control Act of 2011," http://www.cbo.gov/publication/42214 (accessed February 10, 2012).

[28] Department of Defense, "Sustaining U.S. Global Leadership: Priorities for 21st Century Defense."

[29] Nancy Montgomery, "USAREUR Commander Says European Mission is Still Vital," *Stars and Stripes* (August 9, 2011); Determination of specific costs is difficult based on the various types of monies used for spending in Europe. Operations and Maintenance, Partnership for Peace, Installation Management, and other fiscal areas all have parts of the Army's spending in Europe. Additionally, most opponents of forces in Europe use total budgetary percentages to indicate excessive spending in Europe. For example, many pundits are fond of citing the percentage of GDP earmarked for NATO spending to contrast U.S. spending with that of its European counterparts. A GAO Report to Senator Daniel Inouye and Senator Tim Johnson, dated September 13, 2010, notes savings of one to two billion dollars over ten years from 2012-2021 should two of the BCT's in Europe be withdrawn. Using this data for extrapolation, it is possible to estimate annual costs for just the 4 BCT's and additional sustainment and aviation units at $600 million to $1.2 billion. This is an extremely rough estimate but provides credence to the estimate by USAREUR.

[30] Mark P. Hertling, "The U.S. Army in Europe: Fighting Above Our Weight Class," Army Magazine (October 2011): 105-108; 30-40% of USAREUR's forces roughly translates to 2 Brigade Combat Teams (BCTs) which is the average level of deployed troops sustained during operations in Iraq and Afghanistan. Following the conclusion of major deployments to Afghanistan in 2014, the remaining 2 BCT's in Europe will be ideally positioned to sustain efforts in Europe.

[31] James G. Stavaridis "Testimony of Admiral James G. Stavaridis, United States Navy, Commander, United States European Command, Before the 112th Congress, 2011," March 2011, http://armed-services.senate.gov/statemnt/2011/03%20March/Stavridis%2003-29-11.pdf (accessed February 4, 2012).

[32] Personal observations of the author based on service with the 2nd Stryker Cavarly Regiment from 2008-2011, and with a first hand knowledge of training and operations between 2 SCR and elements of the Romanian Army.

[33] Andrew Bacevich, "NATO at twilight," *Los Angeles Times, (February 11, 2008),*pp. A.21-A.21, http://search.proquest.com/docview/422190030?accountid=4444 (accessed March 9, 2012).

[34] International Security Forces-Afghanistan Website, "Troop Numbers and Contributions," http://www.isaf.nato.int/troop-numbers-and-contributions/index.php (accessed January 14, 2012).

[35] Personal observation of the author based on experience in Combined Team Uruzgan from 2010-2011.

[36] David Abshire, "NATO Makes the Grade in Libya" Politico.com, August 26, 2011, http://www.politico.com/news/stories/0811/62106.html (accessed January 24, 2012).

[37] Landstuhl Regional Medical Center "Fact Sheet—Trauma Services," October 2010, http://ermc.amedd.army.mil/landstuhl/factsheets.cfm (accessed January 24, 2012).

[38] Ryan C. Hendrickson, "The Miscalculation of NATO's Death," *Parameters, 37*(1), 105. http://search.proquest.com/docview/198030726?accountid=4444 (accessed February 4, 2012)

[39] North Atlantic Treaty Organization, "Press Release: Financial and Economic Data Relating to NATO Defence," March 10, 2011.

[40] North Atlantic Treaty Organization, "Press Release: Financial and Economic Data Relating to NATO Defence," March 10, 2011.

[41] Barack Obama, "Renewing American Leadership," Foreign Affairs 86 (July/August 2007): 2-16.

[42] R. Brent Gallupe and Michael Parent, "The Role of Leadership in Group Support Systems," Group and Decision Negotiation 10 (2001): 405-422.

[43] Samuel P. Huntington, *The Clash of Civilizations and the Remaking of World Order*, (New York: Simon and Schuster, 1996): 312.

[44] George Washington, "Farewell Address," September 1796, http://avalon.law.yale.edu/18th_century/washing.asp (accessed January 24, 2012).

[45] North Atlantic Treaty Organization Web Site, "The North Atlantic Treaty," April 4, 1949, http://www.nato.int/cps/en/natolive/official_text_17120.htm (accessed December 15, 2011).

[46] Richard F. Grimmett, "Instances of Use of United States Armed Forces Abroad, 1798 – 2004," Congressional Research Service, October 5, 2004, http://www.au.af.mil/au/awc/awcgate/crs/rl30172.htm (accessed February 23, 2012).

[47] James G. Stavaridis "Testimony of Admiral James G. Stavaridis, United States Navy, Commander, United States European Command, Before the 112th Congress, 2011," March 2011.

[48] Benjamin H. Friedman, Eugene Gholz, Daryl G. Press, and Harvey M. Sapolsky, "Restraining Order For Strategic Modesty," World Affairs, Fall 2009, pp 84-94.

[49] In addition to the attacks on 9/11, terrorists attacked on U.S. soil in the 1993 bombing of the World Trade Center and attempted attacks on multiple occasions including the "shoe bomber" in 2002 and underwear bomber in 2009. Additionally, the 2010 failed car bombing in New York City indicates a continuing ability of terrorists to attack on American soil.

[50] Steven A. Hildreth, "North Korean Ballistic Missile Threat to the United States," Congressional Research Service Report for Congress, January 24, 2008.

[51] Mark P. Hertling, "The U.S. Army in Europe: Fighting Above Our Weight Class," Army Magazine (October 2011): 105-108.

[52] Based on the author's personal experience. During the author's service in Europe, the 2nd Stryker Cavalry Regiment conducted multiple partner exercises with units of the Republic of Georgia, Romania, and the Czech Republic. In the case of the Romanians, the 2nd Stryker Cavalry Regiment served in Zabul Province, Afghanistan, from 2010-2011 with units with which it trained in Europe.

[53] Eurocorps Web Site, "History of HQ Eurocorps," http://www.eurocorps.org/history.php (accessed February 23, 2012).

[54] North Atlantic Treaty Organization Web Site, "The NATO Response Force," http://www.nato.int/cps/en/natolive/topics_49755.htm?selectedLocale=en (accessed December 15, 2012).

[55] Department of Defense, "Sustaining U.S. Global Leadership: Priorities for 21st Century Defense," (January 2012): 1-8.

[56] Personal observation of the author based on service at both Grafenwoehr, Germany, and Ft. Bragg, North Carolina.

[57] Elizabeth Bumiller and Steven Elranger, "Panetta and Clinton Seek to Reassure Europe on Defense," New York Times, February 4, 2012, http://www.nytimes.com/2012/02/05/world/europe/panetta-clinton-troops-europe.html?scp=1&sq=panetta%20reductions%20in%20europe&st=cse (accessed February 5, 2012).

[58] Global Security.org, "REFORGER," *Global Security*, http://www.globalsecurity.org/military/ops/reforger.htm (accessed February 4, 2012).

[59] Zach Furness and John Tyler, "Fully Automated Simulation Forces (FAFs): A Grand Challenge for Military Training," http://www.mitre.org/work/tech_papers/tech_papers_01/furness_fullyauto/furness_fullyauto.pdf (accessed February 23, 2012).